The Blue Guitar

PADRAIG O'MORAIN

salmonpoetry

Published in 2011 by
Salmon Poetry
Cliffs of Moher, County Clare, Ireland
Website: www.salmonpoetry.com
Email: info@salmonpoetry.com

ISBN 978-1-907056-73-4

COVER IMAGE: *Guitar Strings* © *Bizroug* | *Dreamstime.com*
COVER DESIGN: *Siobhán Hutson*

Salmon Poetry receives financial support from The Arts Council

To Phil, Niamh and Hannah

Acknowledgements

I am grateful to Alison Brackenbury who chose my pamphlet of 20 poems, *You've Been Great*, as a winner in the Poetry Business Awards; to Ann and Peter Sansom of Smith/Doorstop Books who published *You've Been Great*; to Jane Draycott and to Meg Peacocke for their wisdom and encouragement as teachers; and to the editors of the following magazines: *Ambit, Books Ireland, Cinnamon Press* (*Glimmer* anthology), *Cyphers, Éisteach, Navis, Poetry Ireland Review, The Interpreter's House, Magma, The North, The Rialto, ROPES, Snakeskin* (internet) and *Stand*.

Contents

Taking the plunge

The boy in the photo hangs above the Atlantic
like a drop of rain from the edge of a leaf,
paused in mid-air between diving board and water
on tiptoe, arms spread like a dancer, balanced
between this moment and the next.
He seems to delay, motionless,
where delay is forbidden,
where what's permitted is a plunge from past to future.
A camera clicks, he does not hear.
One day he will look at the picture and declare:
That's odd, I don't remember a thing.
Perhaps that dot in mid-fall
was not me at all.

Ancestors

We seldom speak of you in this house
where you stabled your plough horses.
You are that silence between sounds we rarely note.
Are these hedges compositions from your hands?
Did you grunt in these ditches,
dragging out weeds from sucking mud?

We changed what you thought might last
past your time of horses and scythes
– they crumbled, there is neither bone nor rust left –
we sliced off one river bank,
weeds dance in your ditches,
a motorway storms through your High Field.

There are still apple trees, chestnuts, a few primroses.
We carry you in our blood into the fog.

Achilles in the farmyard

He set down a round of ash
with exact concentric rings,
quickened his mind, swung the axe
and cleft the wood so cleanly the halves
stepped apart like dancers.

He'd rather timber that put up a struggle,
gnarls and knots that refused the steel,
made it glance like a sword off a shield.
Once he fancied himself Achilles
in battle sending heroes to the underworld

as he turned the stubborn wood this way
and that, split off the edges that fell easily,
cutting closer to the implacable core.
The block, gripping the axe, rose up.
He crashed it down in a rage.

He crashed it down again. It would not break.
He tugged until the blade was free,
then kicked the block aside and, fretting,
left the yard, like Achilles
having met a thing that would not yield.

Salvation

The doctor's pleasure on Saturdays
was to drive out to the hotel
and behind its ivy-veiled facade
its dark and crimson draperies
to feel up the chambermaids
the *fillies de chambre* he called them
in an unreserved guest room.
At Sunday Mass he took communion
with a little Mona Lisa smirk
and people called him a hypocrite
though he never confessed a sin
and sinned again: he never confessed
but used his power of absolution
for if a maid got into trouble
he'd dispense a cleansing *curettage*
leaving her *in statu quo* he'd say,
exhausted between stained sheets,
and be home in time for tea.

The hairdresser pauses

The hairdresser stands behind me,
her hands flowing over my hair.
We could be under water
in a glass tank, an exhibition
of absorption or of peace,
like the breathing of an accordion
before the first note is played.
On the worktop creams, scissors,
the steriliser hums to itself.
The hairdresser pauses, comb poised.
What are you thinking? I inquire.
She stands in stillness for a time,
then: At the moment I am thinking
of going out for a cigarette
when I am done with yourself.
She makes a last pass with the scissors
and I picture smoke wandering
from her lips up to heaven.

Cut-throat

Sunday tomorrow. The house goes still.
Her father steadies himself at the basin,
foam like January snow on his face.
Her mother holds a finger to her lips.
The child stares at the razor.
They name it a cut-throat
he told her once. She doesn't know why.
He begins. Child and mother hush.
In the yard, calves and donkey fall silent.
He scrapes trails of smooth skin,
rinses blood-pinked foam
off the blade. Job finished.
Her mother holds out the towel. He turns
grinning, once a week clean, innocent
as anything. Yes, her mother says drily
that's the one I married alright.
Then she goes out to get in the turf.
The child hugs her father and breathes in
the benediction of soap and water.
Outside a calf bawls, the donkey calls.
Lightness comes back to the house for now.

The red heifer

The river field sinks into the dark,
raindrops drip from the slates of the cowshed,
the paper sprawls across the kitchen table,
it says it's hot in California.

A cow serenades the night with vulgarity,
a bony sister cow gazes
from the front of the Irish Foreign Missions,
beside her a bony tribesman grins.

My father stares through the kitchen window.
The red heifer tried to get out today, he says,
better fence the gap in that hedge
or she'll be up the main road tomorrow.

Could she make it as far as the city, I wonder
to marvel at buses bigger than ricks of hay,
streets louder than the bull in Walsh's shed,
newsboys bellowing the Herald, the Press

while we search the fields by the road to Dublin,
peering into the deeper ditches,
my father already grieving the heifer
as she halts, bedazzled, on O'Connell Bridge?

Not talking

Since the final fight, details now forgotten,
when pride sealed up their hearts and mouths
they have made their own mute liturgy:
the scraping of a chair announces dinner,
the car engine turning signals Mass.
Today he makes another vow
to renounce their wordless rituals,
drop onto the permafrost of their days
a solitary phrase to skitter across
the hardened ground of their silence
but he is, as usual, afraid
to violate the long silence of the years
with the sacrilege of speech.

Morning blessing

He flits from the butcher's stall across Main Street
unbuttoning his beige coat. The usual need
drives him to Kelleher's discreet side-door
for his morning blessing, large Powers no water.
Kelleher holds the bottle to the measure, pours
and drones on about the price of cattle
while he prepares himself for the awaited
mingling of spirits with mind, blood and flesh.
The wife had hung on wanting to talk nonsense
while he sorted fillets and ribs until the time
she went to her mother, still not right, thank Heaven.
Later she will turn away from the whiskey reek
but now a sunbeam dances in from a blue sky
and the shadows seem to fly. He has another.

A night out

They have made the effort all the same.
Spruced up in fresh, pressed clothes
in the beige of the Corrib Lounge
they share a desperate silence
pretending to listen to their own minds.

Once, words spilled from them like wheat from a sack,
golden as grain in a good year
or they stretched out in a different silence
that lay lazily between sighs,
little enough needing to be said.

Now, they stare ahead and wait for words
like landed fish out of oxygen
but nothing leaps from these tongues tonight.
Yet, in this silence, in this nothing to say,
is there not tenderness, everything said?

The calf-man

Three or four times a year a van drove into the yard,
the calf-man climbed out and unlocked the doors
to show to my father, who pretended scepticism,
two or three calves blinking, lying in straw.
They gawped from the dark of the calf-smelling van;
the calf-man poked them with his stick to get them up.
My father's resistance always unravelled in the end
and the two men prodded a gangly calf to a shed;
then the calf-man came into the kitchen to be paid
towering, reeking of cattle, his dung-stained coat
buttoned tight, his cap scarcely covering his great skull.

He refused tea while my father wrote out the cheque;
they argued a little over the luck money
before he left, the van moving up the hill
past the elm trees, to try his chances in Malones'
and only then, if he thought he had got a bargain
would my father look at us and grin shyly
while outside the calf lifted her head and bellowed loss.

Once off

On a burning childhood day
in that corner of a field
where our small, slow river
arrives from Malones' farm
just where the river bank
swells into a little hill

where once, years ago,
men bare to the waist
laboured in water
to free the river
choked with weeds and silt
and in that corner
a mound of shovelled mud
became a hill

I pulled off my clothes
and ran down the slope
into the meadow.
But beneath the bare sky
a breeze touched my skin
and whispered of discovery:
What will they say if they see?

So I sneaked on my clothes
before I could be caught
and walked home wondering
at my unexpected daring.
I was eleven, maybe ten.
It did not happen again.

War of Independence: unrecorded incident

Willy Murphy is not in the war.
He carts gravel and clay
along the birdsong roads of Kildare,
milks a cow, can shoe a horse
draws turf from the Bog of Allen.
He is not in the war. The Tans do not know this,
nor do they care: all are guilty.
When he hears the lorries stop outside
he leaves his bed at midnight,
flits by the hedge of the field
to the sheltered pond at the far corner, slips in.
He thinks of men dragged behind lorries,
torment in the barracks, an infant shot for sport.
The lorries start up. Engines fade towards the Hill of Caragh.
But sometimes they leave men with guns behind, to wait.
He waits. Mud seeks to suck him into its black mouth
whispers your time came then, you have no business here.
The lorries do not come back.
The dark lightens and a bird sings.
Another day in the story begins.

Influenza, 1920

The dying woman roars again
and the stench of lavender and disinfectant
attacks their revolted senses.
Her awful roaring tears through the bedrooms
and echoes through the great floors below
down into the dark cellar
where their father sketched a dragon
across the wall for the children at Halloween.
Her roars hammer at the children's heads
and terror stains the deepest well of their minds.
The influenza will fling her howling
she believes into everlasting hellfire
and though she is a guiltless woman
she roars in her delirium
for God to pardon her and cleanse her soul.
Her pallid husband goes in and out of the room.
The women shush the children away
for fear they will tumble with her into the pit.
The softness in her voice is gone;
its hard horror dries up their mouths.
The cattle bellow in the yard outside
and the doctor's Model-T Ford
importantly rat-a-tats up the avenue.
The gravel patiently awaits
the wheels of the inevitable hearse.
The women drink tea but fear drives taste away.
They reek of disinfectant and lavender.
They long for fresh air, trees and flowers,
a man yoking a horse to go to the fields.
The dying woman roars again: forgive me!
Her children press their hands over their ears
but now it is too late for that:
her terror has begun to ring
and echo down the passage to their graves.

Primroses

In every room the ring of iron on iron.
My father crafts our house out of a stable.
Horses steam and stamp in next year's parlour.
He balances on the ladder shaping
the loft into a floor with three bedrooms.
Pausing, he looks across the fields to Caragh
and his heart flies over hedges to his bride.
While apples fatten on the trees and fall
he gouges windows out of hard-yielding walls
and does not pause for rest until spring
when primroses wink at him from the banks
and make him laugh at the good of it all.

The new calf

My father knots a rope behind the calf's hooves
– only the hooves have come out so far – tells me: Pull!
The cow jumps and bellows, the calf seems to resist,
my arms are hurting. It's no use, my father cries
but I strain at the rope until my hands burn.
A nose appears: the cow could do all this herself,
the ears are out but my father calls: Keep pulling!
At last the glistening calf drops onto the dung.
My father unties the knot, slaps him into life.
The cow inclines her head and licks until he kicks.
Not a bother on him, my father appraises.
I drag across the yard to my room and my homework
Julius Caesar, the Gallic Wars, in a dead language.
The calf sways and digs at the udder for milk.

The raconteur

His jokes drew titters
from his audience
of country people,
his style too:
his tweeded cuffs,
his horsey trousers,
Brylcreemed hair,
that rakish leer,
sneer, and grin,
a John Player
dangling from his lip
though he airily
swung it away
to sip whiskey
or sing a verse.
By the mantelpiece
he held us all
with cunning quips,
digs wrapped in jests
but felt as digs.
In early morning
when birds were awake
he slipped into his
shiny Prefect.
He left in the air
a whiff of cigarettes
and Jameson
and cold laughter.

The trouble with chipmunks

'A chipmunk is not an attractive thing.
That odd little roly poly body,
those long teeth gleaming like stainless steel,
could not bring success on the social circuit.'

As he spoke he glanced around the group
already bored, loooking for another drink.
What are they good for anyhow? someone asked
but he ploughed on with his unwanted chatter.

'Chipmunks dance to catch up
from the margin, wild eyed, struggling
to salvage their dignity and their okayness
and not be undesired and unregarded things.'

There was nothing any of us cared to say.
We drifted off or talked of something else
and left him looking at his shoes,
grinning from his place on the edge.

You've been great

A bronzed man pirouettes
on the TV in the corner
for his afternoon audience
in the nation's dayrooms.
They ignore his antics.
They are viewing re-runs
of home movies in their heads.
He spins faster and faster.
Still no-one one takes an interest.
He cracks a joke, he titters,
he says you've been great and winks
at what he thinks is his audience
of frustrated housewives.
Someone says see you soon.
A medicine trolley rattles.

Roadside memorials

From time to time relatives visit
as if they expect the spirit
to have been too shocked to leave.
Sometimes they whisper around these memorials:
'I was first to find them'
'I opened the door of the car'
'I have never forgotten the silence'.
Now and then a robin lands at the feet
of the small statue of Our Lady
to crush a snail's shell
get to the soft flesh inside.
Stones shot from speeding wheels
split her nose, her eyes.
The relatives will stop coming,
rain nudge broken statue and plastic flowers
into the ditch and common earth,
only wind and tyres sigh by
the lost wound in the motorway.

Stronger than death

Death said hello to the boy from the farm
in a city market blaring with clatter
where his aunt haggled until, like a shadow
a man, whispering, appeared at her side.
All stopped. They hurtled back to Caragh.
Now he knew what death meant: bad news flying
up the line, women hurrying home.
He longed for Ladytown. Since death sidled up,
he felt as if he had been gone forever.
A key clicked in the door. His mother.
He would never forget his delight
that one stronger than death had arrived
to take him from this knowledge and this place.

Lambing time

You could read a book in this light! the boy cried
laughing at how the moon lit up the field
as his father moved softly from sheep to sheep
as they gave birth in the brilliant moonlight
to glistening lambs who got a lick from the ewes
and shook themselves as if they had no time to lose
and went straight for the teat and got down to work
and it was like magic, like something in a book
to the wondering boy who knew nothing yet
of the hour of terror in the abbatoir
of machines for driving spikes through heads
of blood darkening on tiled floors
under brilliant slaughterhouse lights.

With Niamh in Harcourt Street Children's Hospital

The intravenous drip machine doggedly
hums through the night,
breaks into fits of frantic ticks
as if it wants to fight its way out of the room.
I have my comforts: book, newspaper, flask of tea
and most importantly: a naggin in my briefcase.
A child wails on the wards, always;
shoes clack on tiles;
you, inscrutably
suck on your soother;
I eye the briefcase.

Beginning of time

Niamh realises suddenly
she is not, after all, ready
for Montessori and all that.
She lies down in the hall,
howls until I grab her
and bundle her to the car.
As she is driven off
I say the words for her:

From now I am ruled by clocks.
When they have finished with me
I will be past recalling
the timeless days without end
that you ended this morning.
The car has slipped round the turn.
I hurry inside to my desk
and begin, the thing done.

Last dance

A knot loosening in his brain
has closed the book of expectation.

He shuffles for miles in purple tracksuit bottoms,
mumbles the thing again and again.

What comes out of his mouth defies meaning:
what matter now are words already spoken.

The suits have gone to the charity shop
but for one that will do later.

The job was good, they let her keep his car
it sits in the driveway looking big.

He dines on scrambled eggs and meat cut up small,
the same for her, she can't be bothered.

The bedroom-slipper shimmy the nightly dance,
she catches him on the street trotting home to mother

and partners him back to the room
the smell of cigarettes and disinfectant.

While she sleeps he shuttles between lock and lock
muttering the thing is, some step to be taken, but what?

The blue guitar

When the blue guitar came
your dolls had already
become strangers to your hands
slipping without complaint
into the lost corners of childhood.

You picked out the first sounds
and I recalled suddenly
your blue dress catching the sun
as you skipped and sang in a gaggle
of small girls in the playground.

Soon you will skip out of this street
the blue guitar on your back
humming your own melody
looking for your new address.
I will turn and catch the dolls staring.

Watching you walk to work

I watch you walk down the South Circular Road.
In dappled shadows, leaves and sunshine
you seem to dissolve into dancing dark and light,
before you vanish in the bright distance
into your efficient world of telephones,
enquiries and tomorrow's appointments.
I imagine this: without warning, sunlight
surges into the room where you do your work,
illuminates desk, keyboard and filing cabinet
and touches the morning's urgency with delight.
I see your head bent over lines in databases,
and I picture you after school perched up a tree
in Long Eaton, smoking and giggling, a thread
of illicit blue smoke curling through the green.

The otter

The otter stuck a coal-black head out of the water.
He was the first I'd seen. He glared with a cross face
then, as if in a hurry, in a sudden dive, went under.

The river, brown with clay from a weekend's rain,
had washed this otter from his hunting ground
to the city's edge. He looked up at me again.

My father used to say the otter will bite
a man's leg until he hears the bones crunch
so fill your boots with cinders to trick him.

The day after he was gone. I hoped he had not sailed
the wrong way, past the Isle of Man ferry,
to the wide sea which had no home for him.

Sometimes his face looks up at me still
and I think of cinders in fishermen's boots
and floods that sweep the certain world away.

The light in winter

January: the tips of bushes
brighten with an icy glow

that loans a sheen of spring
to a tree with a hardened apple

pockmarked by a robin's beak
its skin mottled by the frost.

Dusk turns colour to shadow.
In quietness I wait and watch

the trees grow into stillness.
The light in my house seems to shrink

from the embrace of darkness
its dead heart, its chill breath.

The voyeur at lunchtime

While he watches intently she smirks
and, poised on a much-worn carpet,
she raises a leg, slips off a shoe,
then the other, lustrous, crimson
passes them to him to hold and stroke.
She grins while she opens her jacket.
Behind her a new radio plays
My Love is Like a Red Red Rose.
He folds her teeshirt over his lap.
Outside somebody hammers metal.
She undoes her jeans, tosses them to him.
He touches her heat in the creases.
A woman laughs somewhere upstairs.
Her brassiere is light as tissue.
The sofa creaks. Her fingers flutter.
He watches, alert and silent
but for his breath rolling through the room.
She finishes up with a titter.
He fumbles her the money and her clothes.
One says: Until the next time so.
He sighs and goes into the clanging,
ringing, roaring afternoon.

The petrol pump attendant

He stares again at oil in a rain puddle,
kingfisher streaks, blue and green and gold.
He's seen this kaleidoscope so many times
he cannot admire the colours anymore
and mostly the oil reminds him of shoes
while the hours from two to ten inch on
not even hours, the one hour grinding over
and over – except for a day when his boss,
sporting a pair of flashy cream shoes,
stepped out of the car into the oily puddle
and effed and blinded to his dainty wife
"A hundred and twenty five pounds, the hoors!"
and kept on yelling it like a shout of grief
"A hundred and twenty five hooring pounds!"
Except for that one day the hour drags on
time spreadeagled over dirty ground.

Me and my shadow

Could we explore my shadow? I asked
my shrink. She laughed, said Look,
this is worse than the truth about Santa
or God but I feel I ought to tell you:
You are stuck, I am sorry to say,
with the grey man who carries your name
because you have no shadow
from a scientific point of view
no matter what your man Jung may have said,
tobacco-smelling old goat.
Work it out: why should there be a playboy,
a James Bond who enjoys girls
with golden skin in every port,
not common but sophisticates,
sassy princesses and female spies
yet exists as your shadow
while you wait for the lights to turn green
beneath rain clouds, in your Honda Civic,
drink wine from Spar, bed by eleven
then get up next day to do it again?
All this while your leering shadow cavorts
in Monaco and Monte Carlo?
Sorry, this is no place of dreams.
Now, back to your anxiety.

A minotaur in Manchester

You don't get goats in Manchester
but Sandra's house in the sombre city
has a Mediterranean theme
that reminds me of Crete at sunset,
a whiff of oranges, clink of goat bells,
a bull roaring in a labyrinth, even.

It would be fun to send goats to wander
by Lambeth Avenue's polite houses
bleating and tinkling, devouring privets,
pillaging their way down Roman Road
to the cemetery on Sunday morning
to feast on flowers and funeral wreaths.

And the bull comes thundering through the gates.
Relatives and goats take to their heels and bolt
down the neat and gravelled walks.
The bull barges into an alderman's vault
he wants his labyrinth, familiar ground,
and disappears, but every now and then

with a roar from below, a shudder of earth,
flings bones dancing into the air
and his big yellow horns thrust and pound
then vanish until the next eruption so loud
you could no longer hear a goat bell tinkle
or lawnmowers whirr in Oldham's ordered gardens.

Jesus loves Angela

Angela da Foligno, Italian mystic, died 1309

It began on the beautiful day,
Angela called it, the beautiful day
an angel whispered to her on the Newbridge road:
A message from Christ: You make my heart burn.

Three days later Christ called round himself.
He played hide and seek. He hid under beds,
behind the curtains, tickled her, hid again
until she collapsed exhausted, giggling.

Once she dreamt she was with him in the tomb
for a blissful night before he rose.
Angela stroked him, kissed him, embraced him.
What else, she asked us, could she have done?

She wanted us to crucify her
so she could share his passion, his pain.
We laughed until we found her in the church
spreadeagled naked against the cross.

Her husband hauled her to a doctor
off the telly, cost a fortune,
put her on tablets. She lodged them
behind her teeth, then spat them to the dog.

When himself and the child were killed
by a hit and run on the Newbridge road
she tittered it meant more time for Jesus
and dressed as a bride for the funeral.

It seems unfair: she died in bed, an old woman
unpunished, sins confessed, absolved.
At the end she gawked at the curtains
and then she giggled, and was gone.

A man across the square

There it is: a little flash like a hello and the man
is back. He studies her through field glasses
from a window across the rectangle.
She thinks it's a man: it is a thing men do to women.

> His steady binoculars create a quickening
> in her blood when they glint.
> She pictures him witnessing, implacable
> behind the glasses, getting the full picture

across the distance. This joins them,
his seeing, his intentness, what electricity burns
through his brain while he watches her.

She peers across at that wall of eyes.
What does the man who spies on her see?
Only her evening self sipping wine,
nothing forbidden. Buy glasses? Look back?

> Perhaps she will, she decides, when she's old
> like that lady below on her patio,
> waters her roses and never looks up.
> For now she sits here known and not alone.

Now her comings and her goings matter
to a man whose need reaches into her room.
That feels like enough for her.

And when her witness is gone, if he goes before her,
and the lens no longer glints. Then what?
Ought she tend roses or become a fierce
old woman with a small dog

that she will trot to the park every morning
– or maybe a Papillon that will fit in her basket –
then sit in front of the museum and talk
to other old ladies with small dogs?

Yes, she could buy binoculars and stare back
at his window, scare him away.
But then the silence across the square?

War talk at the barber's, 2003

Will there be a war Jim? the barber asks
as he flicks snips of hair off Jim's shoulders.
Jim tugs at his jacket, makes it straight,
carefully flicks another hair away,
stares in the mirror as if worried
a part of him might have disappeared.
He picks up a hat, a feather in the band.
I see you're wearing a hat, says the barber.
Jim holds the hat poised between his fingers.
There's a history to that hat, he says,
loudly enough for us all to hear.
Four years ago we went to Bray for the day.
I hate hot weather but the wife insisted
and the sun scorched the crown of my head.
He glances at the barber. You might remember.
Sure you were like a tomato Jim.
I never used to wear a hat, you know,
but the sun won't touch my head again.
His voice is hushed as if repeating a prayer.
Like them, what do you call them? He pauses.
The barber looks to his assistant
who has stopped clipping my hair to watch.
Sikhs, he says. That's it, the barber says,
Never take off the turban. No good to me,
don't believe in haircuts. He sweeps up Jim's hair.
Of course, Jim says, staring at the mirror,
when I'm in the shade I leave it off.
He stops, looks at us. More like Arabs,
the assistant says. He nods at the TV.
Jim puts the hat on, fixes the angle.
I'd say there'll be a war alright, he says.
That's the way, Jim, the barber says, still sweeping.

A letter from John Morrin, Royal Air Force base, Aden.

Khormaksar, 28th October 1949.
The heat in this place thins the blood.
The doctor says watch out for colds
for six months after going home.
We've a church on camp for Mass
on days of obligation. At night
the Irish fellows say a Rosary.
How are prices at home this year?
Will fattened cattle hold their own?
Demand was not great at Ballsbridge I'm told.
Your letter was the first I heard
about that man's brother going missing.
Perhaps he'll turn up safe somewhere,
though it looks as if the Guards in Naas
are holding out no hope of that.
A lad who crashed-landed in the desert here
was stripped and killed by the natives. I hope
your winter won't be too severe.
I reckon fodder will be scarce,
you will need as much as you can buy
without being burdened with cattle of mine.
It was good of you to keep them for me.
Have you any photos of our old place?
I think of it often out here. It's so hot
I hardly need to lick the stamp.
If I could have them just to see
I'd post them to you by return.
The ones of Lil, yourself, Pat,
made me anxious to be back.

Bodies in the machine

He must have put in his nights in this chair
in front of the Bakelite wireless and smoked
while nettles clustered in his front porch
like eager visitors denied admission
though a young ash had sprung up brazenly
in his bedroom, waving out the window
even while he snored, here, out for the count.

Do you want to see his bedroom? No?
Well, the bed sags in the middle,
no sheets smelling of the wash, no woman's touch,
his cap, the pattern grimed, waits on the headboard.
In a blotched photograph his parents
worry. They wonder, perhaps, what a tree
is doing in their strange boy's bedroom.

Sit in the chair in front of the radio.
Its fabric, white the day he bought it,
looks brown as a fingernail from nicotine.
Surely it can't still work? Turn the knob.
A little shock as music gushes out on long wave,
jazz from Marseilles to make young men and women
dance until wine smelling mouths collide.

This was where he went while the damp ate the walls,
nettles crowded impertinently in the porch
and ogled warm breathings, close kisses
while he drank Powers whiskey and smoked, eyes closed,
his closest company the cattle in Moore's field,
until he slumped to sleep in Marseilles lulled
by soft bodies embracing in the machine.

Goddess

When she slams the door behind us
howling
we sit on the iron bench in our back yard
wait, talk.
Over the sound of things smashing he tells fables
I beg for
every time, wanting to wile away as he puts it
the hour
until, her spirit chastened by the empty house,
she lets us in.

A goddess up there in the sky loses her temper
every night
he says. She must never find us
– *Ah the thrill* –
that's why darkness falls, so she
can't see
you or me or the dog, even your mother
down here.
That light scurrying across the sky is a little planet
running to hide.

Those stars, he says, are really scattered
diamonds
from her necklace that she flings across the universe
in a rage
like when your mother flung the pearls
skittering
across the floor, that hard black floor
then cried
until we gathered them all and put them
in the tin box.

And then our back door clicks. She whispers,
frightened.
At least ghosts stay away from this house,
your mother
scares them, my father says with a little laugh.
Now sleep.
Later their voices sound like planets sighing
then silence.
She starts to snore like a faraway storm. I fall asleep and dream
of diamonds.

Behind the door

Careful. If you tilt that bust of Sigmund Freud
a panel may slide open unexpectedly,
in the shadows an obscene cry.
Whatever you do stay out of that cellar:
you may be shocked at who you find in there

frolicking in your basement, all decency gone
as if their straitjackets had never been put on.
Uncle and aunt cast off their conscience with their clothes
do what they should not do with those they should not do it with
under your nose. Keep your distance. But no,

you press an ear tight against that door,
a longing to transgress grows in you
an urge to dare to cross a line.
Your grandfather's grandfather clock tick tocks.
Behind the woodwork something paws.

Down the road

The boy with the shiny laser sword
cuts down father and mother.
Their blood spurts satisfactorily,
crimsons the splashing pool
they bought to make up
for the time Mum went too far.
They laugh. Until he finds his sister
playing naked in his pool
and thrusts with his flashing sword.
Her blood glows gaily red on skin
like scarlet berries on granny's lillies.
She'll stay out of it after that.

He goes to stay with granny
who keeps him in her parlour.
Lilies burn in its darkness,
pale as her fingers.
He waits at her window
knowing pain may bring reward,
bruises are black with knowledge.
In granny's garden a ruby rose,
he cuts his thumb to the bone
on a thorn, swallows blood and stares
down the road, past the houses
where the world lies white, intact.

Something wrong

Fish scales cascade across the draining board
like oily coins thrown by a dismissive hand.
Spotless dishes cram the sink, all innocence.
This makes no sense under these circumstances
no more than the dartboard beside the window
of the tiny kitchen, a man's kitchen.
Build a picture, put a shape on things. Chalk helps.
A fretful quiet has settled over the scene.
You're wondering what went down the plughole.
It makes no difference now. This kitchen
grows old with silence while we stare.
From his chair he'd aim at dead centre
through the kitchen door when he was pie-eyed,
we guess from a dart among the empties.
Here is the note he scratched on the wallpaper:
What I thought was substance was the shadow.
Not a word about fish scales. Time to pack it in.

A good year

Bells. All in all a good year. The callers,
a council candidate, talced and blonde,
the Legion of Mary men, the Mormons
had lingered, his Christmas decorations
a talking point. Why put them away?
Their fading reds and yellows cheered him up.
Oh they all agreed. Sourness too: that girl
from back home, sweating up the stairs, sent
with the news, looked too like the mother
her closed, tight smile, darting eyes. Noting details:
bunting still up in July, his skin so white
that garish carpet from the jumble sale
might have drained its colours from his veins.
The eyes blinked: a picture of a boy,
chest bare. Him as a lad. She wouldn't know.
He saw her building the story
to carry home. He thanked her coldly,
clicked the door shut in her face.
Bells. The street lay dead. Auld Lang Syne drifted
from the flat below. Someone cheered.
He raised a glass to the office block
that hid the stars, the next year coming on.

The labyrinth

I never wanted the black vase. You knew that. The bull
trapped in the labyrinth that wound around its sides caught
your heart, your man's heart, you would not hear reason. No
way out but to haul it all the way from Crete, charming
it past the air hostesses your special triumph.

The vase starred in your story of our honeymoon. I
flung rose, lily, iris into its throat, its cold throat
opening to darkness until I gave up. Nothing
filled it, a let-down, never satisfied. Even
when I cracked it you would not hear sense. It must stay.

Unfair to haul you back last year, already wandering
the maze of memory, no signpost to the present.
You maundered off to buy the vase, the shop no longer there.
I found you gawping in the square lost, making no sense,
my triumph this time to get you on the plane.

I have walked this labyrinth for years, never
finding the key of the door to daylight only
the bull trapped in the dark, the senseless bull choked
with parching dust. When they came from the home
they asked for a much-loved object. I sent the vase.

Slipping in

Dayroom. I watch them meet again in the middle.
'I don't like small apples,' he says. 'I likes them big and round.'
'Daddy is waiting at the boathouse,' she says. 'We must go down.'

A woman I used to know squints at me from her chair.
She blinks with her usual just-discovered concern.
'Have you been looked after?' she asks again.

In the photo I hold up in front of her face
she raises a glass of champagne and laughs.
Hoping for a different answer, 'Is that you?' I ask.

'It must be,' she says. 'Have you been looked after?'
'I don't like small apples. I likes them big and round.''
'Daddy is at the boathouse. We really must go down.'

I'd like to go down to the boathouse,
float by water past ancient beech, a girl
sipping champagne and laughing on my knee.

Daddy stops rowing and turns to us
'I'm glad you two finally came down.'
He grins: 'Try the apples. They're rotten but they're big and round.'

It is getting dark in the house of repetitions.
'Have you been looked after?' she asks with a sudden frown.
Visiting time is over. Too late to get out now.

After winter, spring

The last day of decorum,
they kept the curtains closed
as though he could still insist.

Next day mother and daughter strode
out of mourning, high heels, red soles
skirts swinging above the knee.

That night, curtains flung apart,
they leaped and pranced like cattle
let out to the fields after winter.

Then they stopped. He stood
in shadow, pale, stiff
with rage, fist up, snarling.

The girl jabbed a finger
through his ribs. They giggled
and hip-hopped into Spring.

A drunk woman on the train, resentful

The carriage lurches. My breath is sour with whiskey.
The six thirty slips between snow-covered banks
like he slipped in at the hotel all precise
fingers and gasps where I craved filthy passion.
After, from his briefcase, two miniature reds,
vinegary, tepid. Then, mouth sprayed with spearmint
he steered home sober to my perfect sister
with the shopping, two lamb cutlets
cooled in the minibar while he did me.

Daddy's favourite, Mummy's lovely girl
seven straight As in the Leaving
while I slutted around the town
though all I did then was kiss two boys
and get drunk three times. That was enough for them.
Her wedding, white of course, was the last straw:
Who do you think you are to ruin my day?
And then her neat and proper man:
Perhaps you'd like to leave. I left.

Thank god for that off-licence, the grace
of an anaesthetic for the train
while it slides through fields cold with virtue
before the melt when the muck shows through.
I finished my naggin by Mullingar.
I need a drink but the bar is full
of leering men crowding the corridor
hoping the haunches of women
will brush against them as the train sways.

I got invited once to their cold new home,
a few drinks to shield against expected disapproval.
Her eyes frosted as she smelled my stinking breath.
Then she turned her back. Pride before the fall.
Still, I shouldn't have slipped my knickers
in with the chops for her to find.
I would text but I am out of credit.
The men in the bar carouse in full throat.
The carriage lurches again. Time to join them.

Poison

I watch him take his lunchbox from his car,
make for her house, walk in without a glance.
He is afraid to meet my scorned eye,
stiff as a brick in those pressed pants,
those manly shirts she kits him out in.
The cat – my cat – stirs on her sill.
I think of the pair of them, cat and bitch
purring, waiting for my husband to come home.

My cat returns each day here, to his old haunts,
looking for what he can get, no thought
for me who fed him, cleaned up after him,
gave him a warm place to sleep at night.
The poison takes its time, works sneakily
behind the scenes like she did, starts to spread
into the subtlest spaces of her triumph over me.
She goes about in fear for my cat, my husband.

Dog Latin

Canis lupus familiaris. That's dog
in Latin, he'd brag. Too bloody familiar,
she always threw back, resenting his mongrels
who mocked her in their dog thoughts, she suspected,
trailing her as she stomped around finding fault.
They see you as head bitch my darling, he sneered.
Well, someone appreciates me, she'd mutter,
softening for a moment. Then at it again:
When we married I married your bloody dogs.
The barking stopped for weeks after a black fog
stole her spirit, puzzled them into silence.
I have never got anything I wanted
in my life, she cried then. He sniggered. They sighed.
After a month she lifted up her head, smiled:
Well, it should be *canis lupus vulgaris.*
Tails began to wag. Tongues lolled. Dog breath wafted.

English class

A dead fox is deliquescing in the far field.
It makes a blob of russet by the hedge.
My father and I make ever larger circles around it
because he has not buried the fox.
Sometimes the circle takes me into the rath
where it is not wise to disturb the spirits that sleep there ever
resentful
and once near evening I feared the fox would come
padding around a bush towards me
head down, teeth dripping.

Morrin, what is the meaning of to deliquesce?
It's like melting sir.
It's like melting sir. And where would the likes of you find a word
like that?
In Shakespeare, sir.
In Shakespeare, sir? Did you hear that boys? Morrin reads
Shakespeare
and learns words like deliquesce and russet.
What is russet Morrin? It's a colour sir.
What sort of colour, Morrin? Red sir.
What sort of red, Morrin? Like, like the raddle you put on a sheep sir.
Well boys
Morrin likes the word deliquesce but it takes him a long time to get
out the word raddle.
Perhaps too ordinary for this genius? Is that it, Morrin?
No sir.

It's too late for my father to bury it now
and a motorway roars between me and the rath
and the hedge is gone
but I still see a sheen of red, of raddle, of russet on the grass
where the fox did, yes, deliquesce.

Destiny

You look at home here, your bare feet
resting on the low wall of the terrace,
your hair untidy. While you read
you bide your time for something
snugly wrapped up in your future:
a voice, a rustle of clothes, soft fingers,
breath on your face, yours on another's face?
What else lies coiled in the heat from the tiles?
The bricks have grown too hot. You go inside.
A man walks past like a shadow, thinking.

Satan and Mrs Satan

They got it wrong about you, didn't they?
Horns and tail? Whiff of sulphur? Giveaways.
Better a balding head, a plump belly
grey trousers pressed by Mrs Satan.
Easier then to pass for normal.
Ask Mrs and she'd say you were a quiet man,
loves his telly and his armchair. Oh,
she sometimes wishes for a demon lover,
sulphurus, then looks at you remote in hand
mutters *Some chance*, gets out her ironing board.

But now and then she watches you grow still
in the kitchen, thinking you're alone,
eyes like granite, seeing things she cannot know
a house empty now, holes where pictures hung
a wheel spinning uselessly, a glint
in glass, shit in waste ground, a syringe,
a smear of blood in a toilet bowl.
Then you relax, take tea and daintily
buttered toast into the sitting room.
One slice for you. A slice for her.

Traffik

We will cherish your daughter like one of our own.
Thirteen you say? A flower emerging.
Petals not yet unfolded..
For his money he will expect to see blood.

Yes, the money is good for her tender age.
A family man, so kind to his children.
He has a girl her age, his pride, his jewel.
He will squeeze her throat when he comes.

Don't worry, nothing will go wrong for her.
Oh, a room of her own, made for her you could say.
Your girl will always have a smile on her lips.
A night in the long box sees to that.

We would like you to have this camera. The latest.
She will earn it back in the first ten minutes.
Take a nice picture to remember her by.

Aftershock

Bricks scattered like toys after playing,
a pig rooting in a flowerbed,
the cot, the couch, the fireplace buried,
masks hiding the mouths and noses
of men who lift stone from bone,
children sifting ashes for what is broken,
tumbling already out of memory.
What survives: cup, comb, picture frame,
bunting got ready for a festival,
crops waiting in accusing ripeness,
a girl who startles birds to flight and laughs.

After the war

The seller of balloons is waiting
for her neighbours to persuade themselves
to unlock their doors and declare a festival.

The ground is waiting for a skitter of shoes
lighter than her patient, graceless boots
stood in the plaza like an accusation.

Her balloons she thinks are red as hearts.
Her neighbours say they make them think of blood.
They stay inside and turn their radios up full.

A sliver of music gets out. She recalls a dance,
a slightly wild young man, eyes like black cherries
a slur on the tongue, wine on the breath.

Talking of death, he took what she had and left.
She shuffles a heavy foot from left to right.
Something flickers in her heart, a pilot light.

Phoenix Park after Christmas

A snow path stretches into dark between trees.
Workers drive slowly home from the first day back
as though avoiding the traps the year has set for them,
a frosty skid early warning of what might come.

The hills to the south are charcoal smudges
under cloud tinged with pinks and blues.
On the horizon a dot of yellow light
to which someone is heading home, gingerly.

About the Author

Padraig O'Morain's poetry has been published in anthologies and magazines in Ireland and the UK and broadcast on radio. His work gained a Poetry Business award, sponsored by Arts Council England, in 2007 and the twenty winning poems were published as *You've Been Great* (Smith/Doorstop) the following year. He grew up in Ladytown, County Kildare and comes from a family in which poetry has  long been appreciated: his father composed verses in his head while he worked in the fields and his grandfather's poems are still read at family occasions. He lives in Dublin where he works in journalism and psychology. He has an MA in Creative Writing from Lancaster University. He is married with two daughters.